Songs Of Solitude

Songs Of Solitude

Snehaprava Das

BLACK EAGLE BOOKS

BLACK EAGLE BOOKS

7464 Wisdom Lane
Dublin, OH 43016
E-mail: info@blackeaglebooks.org
Website: www.blackeaglebooks.org

First published by
BLACK EAGLE BOOKS, 2019

Songs Of Solitude

Copyright © **Snehaprava Das**

All rights reserved. No part of this publication may be reproduced, stored in a retrieval system, or transmitted, in any form or by any means, electronic, mechanical, photocopying, recording or otherwise without the prior permission of the publisher.

Cover and Interior Design: Ezy's Publication

Library of Congress Control Number: 2019938303
ISBN- 978-1-64560-003-9 (paperback)

Printed in United States of America

For My Beloved Parents

Thus let me live, unseen, unknown;
Thus unlamented let me dye;
Steal from the world, and not a stone
Tell where I lye;
- Alexander Pope

ACKKNOWLEDGEMENTS

I am greatly indebted to my esteemed teacher Prof. Bibhu Prasad Padhi, a poet of international acclaim, who had been a constant source of inspiration to me. I am grateful to him for his valuable suggestions and unstinted support. I extend my sincere thanks to Mr. Satya Pattnaik and Black Eagle Books for approving this collection for publication. I am also thankful to all my friends who had encouraged me to go ahead with this project.

CONTENTS

I Carry a Graveyard inside Me	11
Echo	13
Soliloquy of Moon	15
Nights of Permanence	17
Deception Point	18
Painted Shadows	20
Why is it So?	22
Prisoners of Birth	24
I Cannot Say Why	25
The Noon the Storm Came	26
The Secret Book	28
One Day the Mirror Broke	30
After	32
Do Not	33
Dichotomy	34
Yellow Goes Autumn	35
We Live We Die	37
I was wandering like a Doomed Spirit	39
Too Far Gone Out	40
Our Secret	41

Sunday Morning	42
You, Too...	43
Gift-1	45
Gift-2	46
I Do not Want the Whole	47
You may Call it	48
Naming a Wish	49
Race	50
Poetry	52
Beyond Bondages	53
The Night the Tree Fell	54
The Child in Me	55
Dialoguing with Face-Book	56
Your House is Not Mine	57
Dead Words	59
On Winning Battles	60
Lost	61
Pigeons	62
Re-Incarnation	64
Great People	66
I Marvel at the Moon	68
December Magic	69
Damsel of Stone	70
Art's Tyranny	72
Moon and I	74
Walk	75
Where the Search Ends	77

Silhouette	79
Morning Mood	81
Dream Dimensions	83
Winter Dawn	84
Stranger in Own Space	86
Another Spring	87
The Lazy sun	88
Roots	89
Pain	90
Road Closed	91
A Battlefield for a Gift	93
The Mahatma	95
Across from Each Other	96
Ahalya	98
Clouds, Clouds Sailing across the March Sky	99
Fettered Freedom	100
When the Koel Sings in the Chaitra Noon	102
Poetry Looms Everywhere..	104
Changeless	107

I Carry A Graveyard Inside Me

I carry a graveyard inside me
Where lie buried a girl in blue
Who once used to sit by a grand piano
Not understanding much music
But charmed by its fluid magic
She let her novice fingers
Slide on its unfamiliar keys;

I carry a graveyard inside me
Where lies buried a young woman
Underneath the moss tiled floor
One who often smiled secretly
At her reflection in the mirror
Who loved to fall in love
With the sound of the sea
The silence of the boundless blue above
And the mysterious melancholy
In the song of the white dove;

I carry a graveyard inside me
Where lies buried still another woman
Sleeping in peace in a callous coffin

Under a mound covered in sod
Cradling in her selfless arms
The repulsions of her
Own flesh and blood;

In winter afternoons of languid suns
Like some doomed spirits they rise
And sweeping through
The layers of slate-fog
They sneak into my blind chambers
And stand plastered to its bleak walls
Like mute resurrected déjà vu,
The woman with a smile painted
On her selfless lips, the one in the mirror
And the dreaming girl in blue;
But before I could clearly see
And feel them again with and around me
They spiral out of my unfamiliar world
Plunging me into the icy bottom of
A deathless agony.

Echo

They come bounding back
 From the walls of past
 Distant sounds, loud and low
In waves of sonorous echo
A symphony of voices dark and white
Flooding the unfrequented corners of my heart;
From the terrace comes
The stern stentorian voice of a man
Reclining in an easy chair
A woman ringing a bell, blowing a conch
Or singing a prayer;
The lilt in a young woman's voice as she
Practiced at the harmonium
Of a girl in her adolescence
Humming to herself as she embroidered
A rose on a handkerchief
Maneuvering the needle to create magic
With her soft finger tips;
Voices are all around
The laughter and shouts of the boys
From the merry play ground;
Echoes of honeyed whispers

Giggles mildly ringing to the
Tune of the purple notes of
The teen aged evening;
The wild rain rhythm on the window pane
The gentle splat of the dew dripping
To the autumn leaves
The whimpering of an icy wind
And the exuberant strains
Of the summer breeze
Music in the spring's wild colour-burst
That fill the empty drawers
Of my grey closet of frost;
Voices , disembodied but dense
Filling the air for a flitting fragment of time
Drown in a crescendo of silence.

Soliloquy Of Moon

I think I will stop tonight
Orbiting the earth
I will cast off my illusive light
Fling away my mantle of fake-silver
And go crashing down
Into some fuming ocean
I will let its brine torrents
Inundate my primeval dryness
And bring my chasms and deep crevices
Into a flooding fullness;
I think I will stop tonight
Shying away from the scars
On my face
And watch with a stoic calm
My form edging off me
Scrape by scrape
Into a night of perfect blackness;
I would rather plunge into a hollow
Of dark, unredeemed permanence
Than receive the offer of 'rebirth
In installments';

Let the sun lend its brazen benevolence
To some other moon in some other
Patch of the space
Let the earth to fill its empty sky
Discover another moon that would
Not mind hiding its scars
In a borrowed brightness.

Nights Of Permanence

You wake up suddenly in the
Middle of a night and feel your
Crumbling walls plastered in a
Pulsating black
Tiny formless fears creeping out of it
To enter your blood, your breath
And squirm into your heart
Your threadbare blanket of time
You wrap around yourself tight
To escape the liquid fright
And desperately wish a reluctant sun
To make a speedy return
But the sun seems to be acting in collusion
With your oppressive night
Holding purposely back
Its relieving light
You struggle like crazy in your
Shrinking blanket
Like a patient in a straightjacket
But the sun keeps trying your patience
Or, does he prepare you to
Bear its absence
In another night of obtrusive permanence?

Deception Point

A point somewhere
Suspended in space
Neither here, nor there
Too remote to fancy
Too close to touch
Neither yours nor mine
Familiar and faceless
A moment of
Abandoned togetherness
Poised perilously between
Our 'never' and 'always';

A point where you and I
Stand unmoved, still
Caught in a mirror-maze
A hundred identical faces
Our own, but bafflingly strange
Fractured and whole
Stare at us , reflecting moods
That lingered on, and the ones
The treacherous time stole;

A point where we stand
Wrapped around each other
In an unknown misty haze
Watching resignedly
Memories bundling up into
Months years, decades
And centuries crumbling into
Empty, deceptive days.

Painted Shadow

Time, like the sea has its odd way
Of returning things it sweeps away
From our private shore
Perhaps it has its own trick
Of settling some old score
Tossing back at us things we loved once
People and places, unread pages from history
Un-scanned maps of unexplored
Islands under some icy floor;

Solemn shrines of our hope
 Where echoed our colored hymns
Secret caskets treasuring our intimate dreams
Lie scattered in ugly piles on the
Black, sordid sands
Shying away from the reach of our
Now unsure hands;
Because they are not the same what
They once used to be
Before they were robbed and ravaged
By the Time and the sea;
Un-exorcised ghosts rising indolently

From forgotten graves
Sodden salvages of mossy memories
Wrapped in a brackish wetness
A illusive reality framed in a lurid halo,
It is nothing but a painted shadow
Etched on the canvas of our wasted days.

Why It Is So?

Why it is so
When we know
That above our forest of darkness
Stars will never glow
We still wait for the moon to show

Why it is so
When we know
A sultry sunless morning
Will be tirelessly waiting
Outside our wary window
We wait for a luminous breeze to blow;
Amidst the drunken resonance
Of discordant echoes
We wait for the sobering placebo;

Under a sky sullen and grim
We still nurture
Out-of-reach fancies of
Our private dreams;
Why it is so
In a desert of scorching woe
We wait for a river of green to flow;

Why it is so
Our deep longing for the things 'lost forever'
We can never outgrow
Why, knowing it is a vain pursuit
A touch n go
We keep chasing the gold
At the foot of the rainbow?

Prisoners Of Birth

It is not that the jasmines
Do not grow outside the
Spike-topped walls of
The lush, well tended gardens
They too survive the apathy
Of the wilderness,
Both bloom soft and serene
In the same fragrant whiteness
But the tiny patch of the sky above each
And the conspiring stars in it
Happen to make all the difference,
The walled ones climb up the steps
Of the temple to adorn the deity
And the wild ones drop on the forest floor
Shrinking in their exotic anonymity
That is the way things go with us
We are all allotted our own
Little patches of earth,

We sprout, grow and wither in the space
Identified for us
Because we are all prisoners of our birth.

I Cannot Say Why

  I cannot say why, but
You still are a forbidden dream of
My empty nights
A rainbow arched across
My ancient sky;

I cannot say why, but
The wet clouds in mine
Turn to a sparkling velvet of blue
When they sail up to your eyes;

I cannot say why, but
You are still a poem on wanton wings
That through my orchard
Of drying fancies, fragrantly fly;

But I know that the color of
The flowers you had so ardently painted
On my eager face
Will keep tormenting me
 With a black restlessness
For the rest of my days.

The Noon The Storm Came

In one bleak summer noon
A storm whistled into my room
Through the window that overlooked
A vista of choking darkness
The bird in my mute cage broke through
Its door
Flapping its frantic wings
Flew out of the window , circling
Higher and higher and was lost
In the crowd of crazy clouds,
The dust waves spiraled their way to
My unopened shelves and whipped out
The cluster of words
Of their deep slumber

And they came tumbling down
Falling awkwardly one upon other
Then rose, up and up
Hurtling around the room in Frenzied whirls
Till they reached the window and
They too escaped into the dark
Now , after the storm departed
Leaving behind its signature on the rubbles
I sit alone in my void of absurdity
Like some saint in a trance
All spent and emptied.

The Secret Book

I know you are afraid to touch me
In the light of the day
The book that holds your secrets
You would rather open in secret;
So I sit comfortably ensconced
In the cozy corner of your secret shelf
Waiting for the thickening darkness,
That is the time you would pick me up
And let your wishful hands
Caress my un-masked face,
I know you would fondly open
Me, page by page, and pore over
 Its contents
You would let your thirsty eye lingeringly touch
The letters , the pictures
In each chapter that holds our story
On its the passionate pages
You would let your fingers rove over
Our oceans of tears , our volcanoes of sighs
The ringing valleys of our laughter
The mountains of our forbearance
 The truth of our trust and our life of lies;

In your longing arms I would come alive
And you will savour the smell of our love in me
In the somnolence of the cloud-clad night;
I know you will have to put me back
In the hidden shelf before the dawn break
Because I know you are afraid to cast
Even a glance at me in the day light;
I have but no regrets, I don't begrudge
 Receiving my small share of love as a scrape
Of the darkness of your night
I will happily let you have all the sun light
To keep your days without me
Clear and bright!

One Day The Mirror Broke

One day finally the mirror broke
I knew it would, it had to
Because it always showed you
 When I stood before it,
I was nagged with questions
Without answers
What I saw and what I should see
Was I actually metamorphosed
Or I wore you all over me
 And made your reflection my perpetuity;
May be it was a parallax
Formed by the deceptive distance

That had become our destiny;
But the agony is all over now
I would no more strive to hold
Your reflection captive within my frame
I would let it escape to roam free
To get caught in some other mirror
That will never capture an image of me,
But I know the hundreds of broken pieces
Will always reflect the sparkle in your eyes
I will just have to hold them
And manipulate their positions carefully
To flick back the light to
Illumine the opaque voids inside me.

After

What after this
Now that the search
Seemed to have reached its end
There is no more chasing the time
Back and forth
Because at this point
The long-pursued moment
Of half-truth and half-lie
From behind a nebulous blue mist
Of half-dream and half wakefulness
Stares blankly at a forgotten world;
Here at this point there is
No brooding over what was desired
And what was got
What was gained and what was lost;
Here from this point
Looking back at the
Road taken or not taken
Does not make much difference
Whatsoever.....

Do Not...

The sunlight and all colours
Are on the other side, your side
This side is a shadow sector
Here my dreams are made of darkness
Do not trouble them
With your luminescence;

All the music and laughter
Are beyond this line
Her in this segment of solitude
My voices are made of silence
Do not torture the barren tranquility
With your melodious eloquence;

On this side is my woe-ravaged ocean
On yours are the green pleasant plains
Do not act a fake-messiah
With fake compassion
To calm the teary turbulence;

Dichotomy

Do we often see the human in a god
A lover and a lecher
A betrayer and a benefactor
A sinner and a savior,
Do we often see god in a human
A creator and a destroyer
An adorer and a seducer
A messiah and a slaughterer ,
Do we see a demon in a man
Or a man in a demon
Or a god in both
Is the vision real or one
Conjured up by our fancy
Or some deceptive parallax
Imaged in our private twin-mirror?

Yellow Goes Autumn

Each yellow leaf dropping
From its happy height
To the clay-brown sod below
Is a page from the album of
The months of splendor
That once lived here,
Half the pictures there are splotched
By a nostalgic dew,
 And the rest ones flaking fast
Losing their gloss to a mellowing hue;

 Outlined against the
Pale-blue autumn-screen
The silk brushes of the kansh-grass
Wave a frosty goodbye
To the departing green,
Days dwarf under the load
Of the heavy ripeness
The sun slants languidly
On the demure mountains;

Yellow goes autumn
Across the now desolate plains
As the vaporous afternoon
Condenses on the waning window panes,
Yellow goes autumn beyond the hills
Sluggish and slow
To greet the dull days of sangfroid
Draped in a smug screen of snow.

We Live We Die

Sometimes in our waking nights
When the spirit becomes feathery light
We wonder where to let our thought stray
Should we let it take a flight

High up to a sky smoky and dull
To keep company of the pale moon
That huddles alone at a corner
After shedding all its dusts of pearl;
Or should we let it saunter about
The shore of a busy sea
Rushing in and retreating endlessly,
To let it feel the light drag at the ankles
 While trading the yielding sand-floor,
And listen to the sea-wind
Singing in the forest of casuarinas
Some ancient lore;
Often our perplexed thoughts grope blindly
To discover a tiny but exclusive territory
 In the sky, in the shore, or the sea
Often our stray wishes and our

Vulnerable indecisions
 Become our destiny that charters out
A course of delusive comfort
When the truth is that we never learn to
Choose between treachery and trust;
And let the little world we carry within us
Turn into an arena of our
Wrestling passions
That of our numerous sins
 And vague pursuits of salvations,
In our dark world of confused convictions
Every moment we live and die
Every moment we love and lie
And let our calm pretences unleash a tsunami
Or make our storm sit
On the wings of a butterfly;

I Was Wandering Like
A Doomed Spirit

I was wandering like a doomed spirit
Within the cold walls of some grave
Strangled with my own voice
Stifled with millions and millions of
Never-spoken words
Till your fragrant silence
Like the muted memory of a dream
We had once lived,
Stole in through some invisible chink
And flooded the chocking emptiness in me!
I was resurrected then, and
Spreading out my wispy wings
Fluttered out of my cold cage
Into your ever welcoming arms
To re-live the ecstasy
In the warmth of your familiar touch!

Too Far Gone Out

I am too far gone out into
The jungle of dead voices
Where all familiar noises
Are drowned in the stifling echoes
That come recoiling from the dark walls
Of somnolent trees,
I still nurse a desire and
Strain my desperate ears
To detect a faint streak of your
Luminous whisper that may
Cut through this opaque thickness,
But all I hear or believe to hear
Is only the smothered screams
Of my own dying dreams;

Our Secret

The smile that flickers on your lips
Is for the world to see
But the smile that flits in your eyes
Veiled in a blue mystery
Is the one meant only for me
With its mesmeric touch
My slumbering desires
Suddenly come alive
And inside me springs up
A fountain of shimmering poetry,
The silence on my lips is for those
That commune with words
But it speaks volumes without a voice
That fills your world
You are alone in the midst of your crowd
As I am in mine
Moving ever together like two
Parallel lines
Never meeting but never wishing
To bridge the gap between,
Happy to share our own solitudes together
And our shadows and our sunshine;

SUNDAY MORNING

A lazy Sunday morning lolls on the couch in a warm terrace
Still wrapped in last night's mood of extravagance,
 Yet to shed the hangover that looms about it
Sunday morning curls in cozily inhaling the aroma
Of coffee moving around in invisible swirls
Gazing idly at the half-asleep streets
As it lets the drowsy shiver in the early -winter air
Tickle the warmth of recollected fancies ,
Sunday is a caesura in the fast beating notes of time
Sunday morning snuggles in the closed pages
Of the home-work copies lying undisturbed
In the schoolbags
It is a dawn-hour dream extended
That squeezes stubbornly into a lazy
Embrace of half-awakened eyes.

You, Too..

Devi! Why do you choose to return
To this land of demons every year?
Every time you depart after slaying some,
New ones sprout up from their dead
To beguile you with their
False faces and feigned reverence
You have to invent new strategies of war
To vanquish the demons re-made;

They say that you dwell in every woman
And every woman is a Devi within
 Mother Goddess , is not the reverse also true?
Doesn't have a goddess in her
Have something of a woman, too?

So , I pray you Devi
Come here in incognito once
Come in the guise of a woman,
You too could see how naked lust lurks loud
In their unabashed glance;

You too will find the demon prowling
In every street, at every corner, by every door
See the blood-thirst in their eyes
Their debauchery camouflaged in
Their devout- demeanor;

After that, Mother Goddess
Will you not lend your Shakti
To your distressed daughters?
Will you not teach them the art
Of fighting their offenders, and demolish them
And rid this beautiful earth
Off the snobbish, smart monsters?

Gift-1

Here I gift you all my days
All my 'before' s and my 'after' s,
Held captive inside this tiny frame
I gift you my Eternity
Keep it strapped to your wrist
As our dream of a timeless tryst
Though fated never to be together
And therefore never to part
We let our own time settle as a perpetuity
In our undefeated hearts,
To foil Time's strategy
We have designed the art
In our frank denial of the destiny
And its inexorable chart;

Gift-2

Here I gift you
All the 'lives' I am destined to live,
Circling the deathless invisible
Point of Love at its center;
Let your finger slip through
Its shinning circumference,
I gift you with this
My endless Existence
Though fated to stay apart, forever
We live in Love together,
Beyond all human pretence
In this circle of innocence;

I Do Not Want The Whole

I do not want the whole of the sky
Only a slice of it will do
Seen through the window of my lonely room
A handful of sunlight will be enough
To dispel the thick clouds of gloom;
I would love to see
The sad sickle of a moon floating
In my steaming cup of tea
As I lounge in my creaking couch
In the darkness
Listening to the soft patters of shadows
As they come crowding in
From the shore of some forgotten sea;
I would love to sit quiet like this
Living the pause between
The racing thoughts on Time's track
I would wish the pause to become an infinity
Wherefrom there is
No moving forward, no coming back;

You May Call It..

You may call it a chronicle that recounts
how in a methodical precision
through hours of fear, of despair, of envy
of forbearance, and fortitude, and even love
and through little acts of dying,
slice after slice has been
stripped off the wholeness of 'living'
till the transparent bottom line is laid bare,
it is a collection of scattered episodes too
that narrates the wasted efforts
of a travel from a pile of live dust
to a heap of dead ash through
a blank meaninglessness ;
and where to from there?
because the road seems
clumsily bifurcated, and an uncertain choice
awaits to be made,
since this is not supposed to be the end
from here one may be led
towards the luminous void of
an emancipation ultimate
or towards the blind immortality
of countless renewals of the chronicled events
the moving on may be directed;

Naming A Wish

What name could be given to the
Frozen wish under the tightly shut clay lids
Waiting for the huge flames to lick
At it from all sides,
Should it be named ' liberation absolute',
The breaking away from the all base matters
From the elements,
And taking a journey upward on
The wings of the blackly swirling smoke?
Should it be called a ' repeat return',
A drop down ward,
To the cool, sandy shore to salvage
The scattered words for rebuilding
An abandoned poem of love?
Even as the clay turns to ash
Amidst the loud hissing flames
The name still hangs undecided,
Struggling between the ' final freedom'
And 'fettered fruition'
Between the 'ultimate emancipation'
And a 'mortal- immortality'

Race

Faster, faster, a voice prods on
Countless pairs of blind feet fly
On the enormously spreading out
Insane tracks,
 Chasing the 'Vanishing nothings'…
There is not even a moment to waste
Not a breath of pause or rest
Or, take a flitting look back;

.vying, prying, lying, and blundering on
Charged with the power of fear and greed
Unfeeling to the passing days, months and years
Cramming up the changing seasons into one
'Season of Speed';

In the race against Time, Faith and Death
Every moment counts, every single breath,
No eyes for the nature
No ties with the neighbour
Making, breaking, and living
Pretended relationships
Just with a light touch with the finger tip;
Move on, Move on, faster, faster

Urges the whispering command
The blind feet leap and rush ceaselessly on
 Not caring to know where the finish lines lie
Clutching desperately to the belief
That to move is to live, to stop is to die;

Poetry

It descends on us like a translucent dusk
Wearing a smile like a fairy tale
It is a luminous voice that rings inside us
Like the peals of a silver bell
One moment opaque and obscure
Like the secrets of the night
Transparent and clear in the next
Like a halo of light
Hovering between the earth and the sky
A Beauty that has always remained a mystery
A Dream stuck in time,
An Angel of Love is Poetry;

Beyond Bondages

Your smile blooms bright in me like an unwritten poem
The mischief in your eyes twinkle like some starry gem,

Shimmering, slithering two parallel streams
We sing and flow silverly in each other's dreams,

Your magic voice, a multi-hued music of love
Trails to breathe life into me from some paradise above,

Two spheres orbiting one center on pre-chartered paths
Equidistant yet close through all the deaths and re-births,

Though far removed yet united
We live in each other's heart
Beyond all bondages, held by a strange bond
That never lets us part;

The Night The Tree Fell

No one knew when the storm came that night
But in the morning the tall, tough tree had fallen
Wrenched out from the depth of earth
The cluster of roots like the stiff, straggly hair
On a lifeless face, pointed upward
It seemed to be looking with glazed eyes
At something in the obscure sky ;
Bared off its greens that sprawled about
With a couple of half eaten fruits still clinging to it
The tree lay in its unwelcoming patch of earth
And the nest where two birds had settled for ages
Now emptied of its occupants lay stuck
In the dead branches like a tangled mass of twigs,
 The tree knew the birds will never return
And soon for it the time will come to shrivel and then burn;
Perhaps it may find another patch to sprout and grow
And the birds would come swooping back
From a sky it did not know;
It will with its two luscious fruits dangling invitingly
From its lusty foliage might a bird's interest draw
And it will come to settle there with its inevitable mate
Weaving once again another stringy nest of straw;

The Child In Me

The child in me loves to live
In its innocent cave of delight
In the company of the
monochromatic figures of shadow and light,
playing hide and seek with a dream
that lures it from behind
a chequered veil of wrong and right;
For all it cares, it may be an adult night
Or a children's day
It does not wait to choose between, when
prompted by a mood to come out and play;
It builds sand castles on the shores
Of some non-existent sea
To catch a faded kite falling, it bounds
And lurches in guileless glee;
Watches itself in the mirror of water
Curious to see the floating image
That looks strangely familiar, and
Familiarly strange;
The child in me, unfettered and free
Totters precariously along Time's slippery edge
Groping for some invisible firm support
To hold in balance
The 'already gone' ones and the 'yet to come' days;

Dialouging With Face Book

'Face Book, Face Book , advise me please
Because I do not seem to know
Which of my faces should I hide from your page
And which one should I show?'

'Keep your real one for your mirror only, dear
Let the world look at all the rest
Wouldn't you want people to see you
As nothing but your best?'

'Face Book, Face Book, do tell me now
Which of the books should I display?
Should they be my own 'less likable' ones, or
Those that hold borrowed matters, what do you say?'

'Better keep your own ones hidden somewhere
Where the eyes of the world can't reach them,
Display rather the duplicated ones, without a qualm
 And keep stuck to your bold claim,'

'Face Book, Face Book, what would be more wise
To put on your page, a book or a face?
'It is the face dear, that interests us better
So, more of the Face, and everything else, less.'

Your House Is Not Mine

'Come to my house, once,' you say and smile
My answer to that is a smile, too
Since you know as I do
You never want me there and where
You had wanted me in some forgotten time
I can now never go!!
The walled world of yours had
Never been your dream,
As mine too has never been so!!
And who knows it better than I or than you?
In your sunlit world, you live in blackness
And Time pants as it struggles through
Your aging years, months and days…
But, it has been kept stuck
In my permanent 'now', without strife
As I try to steal from every single breath
Life after life!!

Between your world where Time moves
In a desperate whirl
And mine where it stands blank and still
There is a tiny pause, like the one that squeezes in
Between one and another breath,
 There we often meet in a moonlit darkness
 There, where Destiny seems to conspire
With a delusive Life and a defeated Death;

Dead Words

There were days when they bloomed
In sparkling clusters in a sky that we shared
Just between us,
We plucked them out handfuls and handfuls
 And flicked at each other
Savouring the ecstasy of their scintillating touch;
 It is amazing how these days
We keep so assiduously engaged
In weaving artful garbs for the weaning words
That once had shimmered agelessly
Through their transparent naivety;
Now settled on our heap of hypocrisy, and
Reconciled to our days of chosen silence
 We struggle to paint their dying contours
With changing shades of polished pretence;

On Winning Battles

What is war, what is peace
What exactly do you win
What really do you miss,

All battles are fought inside
Between your 'you' and your 'I'
Between the love for the sand
And a wish for the sky,

Once you know how to merge
Your 'You' and your 'I'
And make it just 'us'
All wars will be over without
The signing of a treaty or a truce;

Lost

The cage had to open finally and as it did,
 all my birds, flew out fluttering
ecstatic wings heading for the fragrant orchard
in you, and entered a lightless jungle instead..
Perhaps the long, long confinement had
affected them a little in the head;
So they circled round and round
the thirsty streams, lost and defeated,
Muted, exhausted in their frantic flight,
their feathers drooping wearily through a vain feat
 of scaling the harrowing heights;

Now that they have drifted into the
depth of the jungle far from your sight
far beyond the range of hearing
 to your signaling whistle which they had been
awaiting ever since the century-old yesterday
they know they can never return to
your forbidden garden, because the mysterious
jungle stands between barring the way;

Pigeons

Scanners of the sky swooping to our roofs
Flapping and scattering a grey-black gloss
Who could say why they always choose to
Come down to our homes and live with us?

Carrying in them more of human
Than that of the Nature
They happily flock about our houses,
The simple, innocent creatures;

Negotiating terms between the
Earth below and the sky above
They move inside humanity, building in
Their fragile nests a whole world of love;

Stubborn settlers, not of the jungles
Or branches of the trees
But of the spires of mosque and churches

And of chains of the temple bells
They always find a niche in the civilized buildings
And a place to rest in the concrete corbels;

Sailing through the storms of distrust
That tears apart their space from that of us
They always return, the peace-makers,
 Fluttering on their friendly wings a flag of truce;

We may keep on wondering forever why they
Make such a strange choice
Why prefer a land of dust, smoke, fog and noise
To a world of the tranquil, green rejoice;

If questioned, they might answer in
Their throaty, guttural voice
It is through them the world god has created
And the one man has made, joyfully interface;

Reincarnation

The devotee stood aghast, trembling
 At the unbelievable sight in his front
The seat of the deity was lying empty
Where had he gone?
Disappeared? Stolen, or lost?

Below the seat was sprawled out
A big shadow, scattered in dismal patches
Threatening to crumble at the lightest touch
 The devotee whined in abject despair
Where he would find his god,
 where to go and search?

Had the god he was worshipping for years
Decided to come back taking another form
What place then he would choose to be re-born
A haystack in a stable, a shack in some desert
Or the cold floor of a dark, hostile prison?

Perhaps he got too tired of the wars fought over him
And of people's arrogant claims
Got too tired in his efforts to put an end
To the blasphemous blame-games;

Perhaps he is in two minds now
Whether to stay back, or to make a return
To the fanatic shrines of mortar and stone
In a land writhing under strife and scorn;

He might decide to wait and make his children learn
How foolish it is
To fight over faith and devotion
Or, he might wait till the war here
 Took an apocalyptic turn
Before choosing a new form of incarnation;

Great People

He had opened his eyes to life
In a small, nameless land that was
Not marked in any geographical map
And now existed only in memory!
In a great city of great men
You survive only in your memory
For the land where great men live
Is like the one the gods sojourn,
An inaccessible territory;
Here, great men settle stubborn
Surrounded by the servitors,
Relishing their blandishments,
Manna dripped from their lop-sided smiles
Hidden in the hooded eyes but there
Lurk a mixed mood of pity and contempt;

He has learnt by now he is one amongst
The little people and so has no regret,
  For not finding entry to
The land of the 'Great';
He knows he is a pariah kept off
The world of the 'glorious great'
By an inviolable ban,
He also knows by now that the great ones
Are a little more than god, and
A little less than human;

I Marvel At The Moon

I marvel at the moon that
Climbs down to hang from
The balding branches
Outside my lightless room,
Scattering its pearls about
To light up the layers of gloom;

Outside the crumbling walls of wishes
Somewhere in an invisible hedge,
A lone cricket chants
A note from the past
In an unknown language;

Smiling fairies clad in flouncy clouds
Trail down from above,
Strewing around my cheerless terrace
Twinkling starlets of love;
I marvel at those moonlit moments
That breathe life back to dead dreams,
I marvel at the moon that celebrates
 The rebirth
Singing its silver hymns;

December Magic

December descends sitting on a carpet of fog
Sailing through a mass of grey,
Cheerily waving its wand of ice
All through the shivering way;
Scattering merrily all through the journey
Sparkling specks of snow-dust,
 Caressing the contours of the sulky earth
With fond fingers of frost;

The crafty conjurer sluicing through
The sleety valleys and plains,
Comes to settle wearily outside
My dew-drenched window panes;

The magic month the Messiah chooses
To return to the warm stack of hay,
The magic month that gleams in the kids' eyes
As they wait for the Santa on the sleigh;

Damsel Of Stone

I stand plastered to the pillar of your
Dance-hall all through the dragging day
Waiting and waiting for the lonesome night
To make its mysterious way;

Then, from somewhere a faint music of
Flute comes gently floating in,
And echoes off the massive walls of stone
Rapturous, delicate, thin;

The dark hall of dance is bathed suddenly
In a fragrant resplendence,
As you glance at me, a wave of ambrosia
Floods through my frozen veins;

Guardedly, secretly, I step out from
The towering pillar of stone,
As if under the spell of some magic,
My stiff, rigid limbs spring into motion;

All through the long, ecstatic night
Strange love notes on the flute you play,

And my anklets jingle drunkenly to the tune
As I let my body lurch and sway;

A half-told tale of Love of another age
Of another time, but never forgotten
Comes alive, although you have assumed
Your new form of wood, and
I have turned to a damsel of stone;

(the theme of the poem is based on the devadasi dance-culture of the temple of Lord Jagannath at Puri)

Art's Tyranny

Like a grand monument,
A testament of sculptural magnificence,
A sovereign monarch's 'dream-realized',
That stands majestic on the dead of many,
 The dull but lingering stains of
 blood, sweat, and tear
  that could have spoken how art was tortured
out of poverty, prejudice, and fear
 but remain craftily concealed
in its shady interiors,
a poem too stands on the graves
of the martyred words, that were
cornered and captured in the dark alleys
of some conceiving, dreaming mind,
and are kept huddled in ugly clusters,
each waiting for its turn to be chained
to the 'contemplation- post' and lashed
till it spills out a bloodstained 'sense'
 to fit into the framings of fancy;

A poem, may be a shrine built by a saint,
Too has, its shady interiors touched,
However dull however faint,
 With the blood of the innocent!

 One might wonder if, like the sovereign ruler
a poet is a tyrant too that throttles out
 of the defenseless words,
as many choices to design and paint
his own artful monument;

Moon And I

As I sat by the lone river
That has lost its way to the sea,
The moon came down silently
And stood beside me;

'Oh, I am so alone!' I mumbled
'I wish I were dead,'
'I am alone, too; let us be together'
The moon with a smile, said,

So we sat together
By the riverside, on the soft sand
Sparkling in the starlight,
Listening to each other's silence
In that mesmeric, blue night!

Long, long after from somewhere
A bird sang, announcing
The end of our night,
'I must leave,' the moon said
And walked away, and I watched it
Slowly dissolving in the
Invading sunlight!!!

Walk

You can walk with many
Or with someone you believe your own
or just alone,
you can walk along a straight road
heading for a known or
an unknown destination
and discover to your dismay
yourself at the point of no return
where there is neither a way back
nor a wish to move on;
sometimes you take a circuitous path
walking round and round unendingly
always arriving where you had begun
like your feet are caught in some
invisible chain
 you keep on halting, wondering
and then start again;
it may so happen in the end
while walking on a curved, crooked path
 you stop at some unexpected bend,
believing that the journey is finished
that, finally you have reached!

It is not always so
That you can reach
Wherever you have desired to go,
 walking does not always lead you
to a spot of your choice
where everything ultimately
is fine and fair,
you may walk miles and miles
 and still reach nowhere!!

Where The Search Ends

How could I recover the reluctant words
That lie so deeply stuck
In the morass of human misery
Or, pasted on the ancient wounds
That scarred our beautiful world;
Should I try to pick some from
The piles of poverty shivering
Under tattered blankets,
Or, from the glazed hope peeping
Pathetically from inside the sunken sockets,

Should I let my verse sing of the hatred
That suffers an unquenchable thirst
For innocent blood
Or, of the debacle of a hurricane
An earthquake, or a tsunami-flood;

The massacre of virgin virtues in
The blind alleys of spiritual strife
A farmer's ultimate choice of escaping
An incomplete, unfulfilled life,

Should I look for the words for my poem
In the screams of the dying victims
Of a bloody explosions,
Or, in the staccato shots of slugs
Spraying from the anonymous guns?

Weary and drained out of the futile search
I turned to look inside and found
A few floating languidly
In the dark pool of my thought
'Want to indulge in the luxury of
Poetry-writing', asked me the unhappy lot;

' To sculpt mankind's eternal sorrow,
Do not use us as the tools of your craft,
Weep their tears, suffer their sickness
Live their poverty, die their deaths
Write the song of their unspeakable sorrow
On the unfeeling pages of your heart
That will be the true poetry
That will be the ever-enduring Art!!'

Silhouette

You happen to be happy
While trapped in a room
With many windows
all of which open only to the
Enormous emptiness beyond,
You happen to be happy
Living your missing moments
Warmly rolling in through the
winter-waves to spread across
The tiny pool of lurid light
Between the twin patches
Sprawled darkly under the walls;
You could be happy drifting
Out of your dark patch to enter
The dimly lit, squeezed-in space
Where a shadowy host of
Masquerading marionettes
Perform a jarring, moody act
In synchrony to the rhythms of
some disembodied, floating notes,
to their plunges and surges;
you could still be happy

as they lure you to join the act,
 to become one of the lot
and let yourself maneuvered
 In glad sweeping movements
Towards the swallowing darkness
On the other end
Till you turn into a sad silhouette
Of an unrealized dream;

Morning Mood

A weaning night begins to slip
Softly under a sleek drape of mauve,
Glad butterflies riding on rainbows
Flit around the flowers of love;

A slender stream goes gliding in glee
Across the pleasantly pebbled path
Like a shimmering smile on the lazy lips
Of a still sleepy earth;

As the naughty fingers of a nascent sun
Starts to shift aside the mist-screen,
She sits up blushing, smoothing the creases
On her velvety bedspread of green;

Listening to the morning hymns from
The leafy towers, now low, now loud
Then sweeping melodiously upward and
Float through the maverick clouds;

'Hour to wake up,' she says to herself
'To mop out the smudges of the night,
To draw a new pattern in a new light,
With renewed efforts and fresh hopes
 To design a day of delight,
To discover the wrong and set it right;'

Dream Dimensions

She lives somewhere inside me
Like an ultimate but un-granted wish,
Leaps out of me to disappear into the glass
Every time I stand in front of my mirror
 And gets transformed to You
 It is a puzzle I could never solve,
If You are my truth or I am your dream;
Drifting blindly between
An anonymity and an identity
 I reach out to touch the mysterious parallax
Which something like Truth seems!
My world is shrunken between
Just two dimensions, of real and unreal
I think, you too exist inside your shadow

The Winter Sun

Things are slow these days
Almost an effort to draw apart
The smoke curtains hanging
Heavily on the horizon,
Then trudge laboriously across
A dimly lit vacuum
To sprawl in a pale patch on
The threadbare, beige sheets
On the morose meadows, or on
The roof of some squalid structure,
Eyes half-opened, mind dazed
To take in the leprous pictures of the

Fencing around, with their
Plaster peeled off at places,
Or, the birds that routinely sing
The temple bells that ring,
Gazing at the grim pallour
That to the stray clouds clings;
Then, turn on its side under
The yellowing coverlet
Through a fast fading noon
To wait in half-hope, and in half -despair
For another morning of decay!

Stranger In Own Space

You often live with a crowd of faces
Some smiling, some glum, some grim,
Some, though distant and unknown
You feel a closeness with them
And are almost involuntarily drawn,
There are faces that bear
A semblance of your own
You want to elude them somehow,
But they refuse stubbornly
To leave you alone!
Leaving no way for you
Other than break the mirrors they live in,
Watching them smash into smithereens,
Each imaging some unremembered sin;
Then, you accept with calm resignation
The banishment from your own nativity
That turns to an uncertain isthmus
Between the islands of your hypocrisy
And your genuineness,
To live through the exile like
A stranger in your own space!

Another Spring

Another Spring comes sweeping
Through the dewy cool breeze
Attired glamorously in a
Whiff of green promise,
Tripping lightly across
A mosaic of merry hue
That glimmer under
An awning of fluid blue,
To play its cameo role between
Two exasperatingly long acts
The frosty soliloquy of Winter
And Summer's loud, angry blast;
Knowing well that
It is only an interlude
That will finish fast
But with the happy resolve to bring
Pure entertainment as long as it lasts!

A Lazy Sun ...

A lazy sun, tucked under a
Blanket of fog, is tickled to a
Secret smile as it watches
Winter stealing through
A snow curtain
And step across the smoky
Lines of numerous poems
Written on its misty dusk
And frosty dawn,
 'come on, come on,
Have your days of icy-fun
Soon your happy hibernation
Will be going up in smokes
Once I come out to take
My invincible position;

Roots

Roots are the ultimate reality,
But a slender sapling, like an
Obstinate wish sprouts up
And looks skyward,
To grow into the promising emptiness
Above, to sip in the
Liquid light of life and send it
Seeping down to the shriveling
Roots in the dark depth,
Because returning to the roots
Is an inevitability,
Because it is in the roots
Another life waits to grow up
Into another luminous height;

Pain

Pain has a timeless quality
It can stiffen us with its almost
Tangible permanence;
It can come from an arrow
Pierced to the sole of a foot
Or from nails driven into them,
It may be a tale of today,
Or a yesterday, or of another
Ancient age;
It prevails and will prevail
Like an ultimate blank,
Haunting our intimate
Nights and days;

Road Closed

But for that invisible hand
That held the road-closed sign
Boldly painted against white
Which, I was sure when the
Journey began on a fine sunny morning
Was nowhere in sight,
But loomed up startlingly
Signaling me to take to the turning
 And that was what
Had changed almost everything;
The wheels of the jolly carriage
Loaded with basketfuls of
 My dreaming 'days ahead'
 Skidded dangerously and hurtled on
To the unpromising diversion;
All my tomorrows, ensconced
In the happy baskets, one after another
Were thrown out of it
As the carriage
 Went bumping on the cobbled track
I had never dared thereafter to look back,

A weary traveler, I had clung to the
 Tatty support of the carriage
That   rattled on and on
In an uncertain mood
On that obscure path that lengthened
Unendingly like the thin line
Between 'Knowing the Truth'
And 'Believing Falsehood' ;
Watching helplessly as all my tomorrows
Rolled off the roadsides and were
Buried in their graves of dust
Wondering if a journey always
Ends up like mine
Leaving the traveler wasted and lost;

A Battelefield For A Gift

The soldier returned at last
Ceremoniously clad in the
Spotless tricolor,
He had brought along with him
A special gift for her,
 It was another battlefield
Clustered with haunting hieroglyphics
Of living horror;
Shocked and shattered she stood
Staring at it
Her martyred husband's last gift,
A battlefield, where she was
Caught in the crossfire
Between her truth and a lie
Not knowing what would be
More difficult, to live or to die,
When sickening words of glory
Sacrifice and honour
Were shot at her
Like bullets spraying from some
Invisible source

It was another warfare, her very own,
And was worse!
She watched dumbly
With eyes burning dry
The dream rainbow dissolving
In her mirrored-sky;
In a war against her own loss
And her own frayed nerves
She knows not
What weapons should she use
 What shield
But, determined never to yield
She stands alone in her
Private battlefield,
Nursing resignedly her wounds
Which she knows would
Never stop to bleed,
Still she stands holding her
Dignified head high
Turning her vacant gaze away
From the fading rainbow
In her mirrored-sky;

The Mahatma

A frail figure he was but a tower of strength
Who, in his pursuit of truth could go to any length;
Who said that a battle is not always fought
With a sword, or a grenade or a gun
Even without bloodshed a war could be won;
Who induced fresh confidence when
Our dream of freedom was a sinking sun
And trained us to conquer the enemy with humility,
With love and yet with determination;
A mentor who taught us the meaning of Love and Faith
A man with the courage to face and challenge Death;
A saint who preached to see in every human being
Not anything evil but only the good
Who had envisaged a world founded on
The laws of tolerance and universal brotherhood;
An apostle of peace who had changed a nation's fate
A messiah of love shot to death by a bullet of hate;
A bullet may kill a body, or a voice it can silence
But the Mahatma will live in our hearts forever
And keep on preaching the gospel of nonviolence.

Across From Each Other

Silhouetted against a vignette of ancientness
They stood still, across from each other
On either side of a river called 'forever'
Which gushed out from one 'nowhere'
To reach another;
They stood there, apart and together
Like two dull scars of a wounded past
 Tormented with an unquenchable thirst
While Time slithered on the rushing stream
Carrying on its currents a kaleidoscope
Of numerous broken dreams,
On the ripples imaging
Countless suns, rising and sinking and again returning
Wrapped in shades of crimson, yellow and blue
And life followed life, death too death
In many a mysterious hue;

Seasons of smile and sorrow
Went sweeping through,
'yesterday's slid into 'today's
'today's into treacherous 'tomorrow's,
And, the figures from the past
Burning with an eternity of thirst
Keep waiting on either side of the turgid flow
Enveloped in an ever lengthening shadow
Of an invisible wall of Jericho
That never stopped to grow
Between some strange heaven above
and an unknown hell below;

Ahalya

I would rather not have the curse lifted off me
I would rather lie forlorn, abandoned
Untouched by the holy feet of the savior-god,
I would continue to re-live and repel
That moment of willful surrender
To an arrogant, seducing lord
Receive and return the echoes of protest
Throbbing in my stoned nerves
Surviving on the air thick with
The smell of that forbidden love;
I would rather not wait for another life
But stand agelessly in a dark forest of numbness
That lies beyond a world
Blighted by the wrath of a celibate sage
Where even gods in the name of love
Hesitate not to commit outrage
Where a slight slip off the sainthood
Forced upon the kinds like me
Is more than a sacrilege;

Clouds, Clouds Sailing Across A March-sky

Clouds, clouds puffy white clouds
Wispy, cotton-wool clouds
Sailing across the March sky
Each one, a fleecy white backdrop
And against each, a montage of memories
Wherefrom pictures of past
One after another come sliding by,
To shimmer in a splendorous colour burst
So what, if I stand by this window of gray
Feet fixed, alone and lost...
My clipped wings heavy with a wish to fly
With the clouds in the March sky,
So what, if I exploit nostalgia
With my blank, glazed eyes
  Wishing, wishing, wishing.... To fly
And float with the clouds in the March sky;

Fettered Freedom

In a way we are alike
Since both you and I
Nourish a passion to fly
To scale the heights of an endless sky,

Still, I am often left wondering
How you must be enjoying
The 'taking-off' from the dense greenness
 To spread out in the infinity
Riding in grace
On the scented wind-waves,

Wafted by a sprightly mood
You let your happy-hued wings roll through
Surfing across the ocean of blue,

Yours is one blessed, unbridled spirit
Goes soaring on and on
Mine is but a short journey
In the aerial route chartered out by
Someone else's idea of fun,

I, too, like you sail across the sky
Close to the drifting clouds I fly
Trembling at their tangential touch
I don't know though if I am happy as much,
My movements all the time
Maneuvered within
Someone's chosen space,
Carrying the loads of
The 'dreaming-impossible' on my paper wings
I struggle through my limitedness,
You are one name of Freedom,
An exuberance of exploring the unlimited
A joy-journey unbunded
Reaching out to all directions
Above and ahead,
I am a name for Freedom too,
Another and a different one
It is called charity offered
By the hands that manipulate the spindle
And craftily release the thread!!

When The Koel Sings In The Noon Of Chaitra

The koel has comeback with its song
To settle in the tree outside my window,
To fill again my long-drawn noon
with its melodious presence;
It returns every year in the month of Chaitra
When the season stands uncertainly between
A submissive spring and a stubborn summer;
The frost-bitten notes that had fallen
in sad flakes of brown and gray
and gone sinking into dust,
now rise and make their way
back to the bald branches,
to plaster them with patches of green,
The voice flows in a rhythmic ripple
from a soft low cooing to a soprano shrill
rising and falling and again rising to its peak
as time seems to stand still,
and the voice flows like waves of magic
in a river of music....
Behind my window, in a vacuum of loneliness

Half-uttered, half- smothered wishes
float around, direction less
wafted by a half-hope that neither
has a name nor a face,
 sometimes tainted with an oppressive desire
sometimes heavy with
the laments for a lost love, or for a birth wasted,
Sometimes pristine and pure
 like virgin letters of love, never posted;

Poetry Looms Everywhere

Like the shadow of infinity
It spreads out to either sides of our existence
A benign spirit around us
Poetry looms everywhere
As an invisible permanence;

It sings in the feathered carols
Hidden in the dense foliages of the trees
Scattering itself delightfully
In the calm autumn breeze;
Under a sky that has shed
Its clouds of gloom
Poetry saunters on the riverside
Where kans-grass brushes
Swing in their silky bloom;

Poetry stretches out coyly
On the shimmering river
Echoing its music, soft and subdued
Sweeping through the twilight
 And its purple solitude;

Singing to the moods of requited
And unrequited love,
By the barren river in a desert
Or flitting on the mosaics of silver
Designed upon the blue above,
Poetry trudges through life's
Laborious lanes
In languid steps, registering its untold pains,
Recording the sad tales of the
Struggles for survival, playing the
Music of life in a sluggish strain;

Poetry moves on to loiter in the
Sad corridors of suffering and sickness
Stopping to watch the graying life
The glazed eyes, and the hard lines of torment
On the shrunken, wrinkled face,
the expectant and hungry hands
And the thirst in the eyes
of Poverty and Helplessness;

poetry moves on to the blind alleys
where virgin nights are ravished
by debauchee savages
where truth-tellers are brutally silenced
and terror-teachers gun down
the schools of innocence;

Clad in a spiritual cloak
Poetry totters on with supporting sticks
By the somber hedge
Of a mysterious, noiseless stretch

Hovering, halting, hesitating
Along the paths, trying to choose between
transience and permanence
 between salvation, and life after death
between the ultimate truth and false faith,
vainly struggling to discover immortality
in dark death's heart
Still, Poetry always returns to earth
To celebrate the permanence of art;

Changeless

'You have changed,' we say to each other
 with a smile that flickers like a 'yes'
and add reluctantly, 'there was no choice!'
We are perhaps world's two worst actors
delivering our well rehearsed dialogues
in such ridiculous absurdity
feigning freedom when we are
imprisoned in each other,
and making choices, knowing well
that we are chained to
each other's infinity!

You have not changed, nor have I
nor will we ever change
because we have captivated our worlds
to put them together as one
in our thoughts' secret range;
 and despite all the tricks of the
scheming stars we will live in each other
as changeless immortality
through the endless cycles of life,
 death, and all the lives and deaths after!!

www.ingramcontent.com/pod-product-compliance
Lightning Source LLC
Chambersburg PA
CBHW052103070526
44584CB00017B/2314